The Nature Kid's Guide to
PIRANHAS

DAVID ANDERSON

LP Media Inc. Publishing

For information address LP Media Inc. Publishing,
30012 Variolite St NW, Princeton MN 55371
www.lpmedia.org

Publication Data

Piranhas
The Nature Kid's Guide to Piranhas — First edition.

Summary: "Learn all about Piranhas, the Nature Kid Way"
— Provided by publisher.

ISBN: 979-8-89818-220-5

[1. Piranhas – Non-Fiction] I. Title.

Title: The Nature Kid's Guide to Piranhas

CONTENTS

RIVER HOMES

The word piranha means 'tooth fish' in Tupi, a language spoken by native people in Brazil.

Splash! A piranha zips through the warm, brown river.

Something moves beneath the surface of a dark South American river. It has razor-sharp teeth, lightning-fast reflexes, and one of the most feared names in the animal kingdom. Meet the piranha!

These fish call warm, murky rivers home. Flooded forests, tangled roots, and dim underwater hideouts are their territory. They know every shadow.

Red-bellied piranhas are the most famous kind. Their glowing crimson bellies flash like a warning in the dark water. This is their river — and they rule it.

FIND THEM

Some piranhas live in water so dark and muddy you cannot see your own hand in front of your face!

Swoosh! A caribe piranha races through a river in Venezuela.

Piranhas live only in South America. Most swim in the Amazon River and its streams. That is the biggest river system on Earth!

You can find them in Brazil, Peru, and Colombia. Some live as far south as Argentina. The caribe piranha swims in rivers across Venezuela, where locals know it well.

Piranhas live in many different habitats. Some prefer clear, rocky streams. Others swim in wide, slow rivers where the water barely moves.

SMALL STUFF
FUN FACT!
The São Francisco piranha is one of the heaviest at nearly 7 lbs!
8

Snap! A gold piranha swims past a rock, flashing its fins.

Most piranhas are about the size of a grown-up's hand. They grow 6 to 10 inches long; shorter than a ruler.

Gold piranhas can grow a bit bigger, reaching around 12 inches. But they are not the largest piranha of all. That title belongs to the black piranha, which can grow up to 18 inches!

A piranha is built for speed, not size. Its flat, oval body helps it cut through water fast. It may be small, but every inch is packed with muscle.

TERRIFIC TEETH

Piranhas lose and regrow their teeth in whole rows at once, not one tooth at a time like sharks.

Chomp! A piranha opens its mouth and shows its razor-sharp teeth.

Piranhas have rows of sharp, pointed teeth that fit together like puzzle pieces. Each tooth is shaped like a tiny triangle with razor-thin edges. When they bite down, the teeth lock tight and nothing slips free. That grip is nearly impossible to escape.

Black piranhas have the strongest bite of any fish their size — generating a force more than 30 times their own body weight. They can crunch through bone, shell, and tough river vegetation with ease.

SUPER SNIFFERS

Piranhas have nostrils, but they use them only for smelling—they breathe through their gills instead!

Sniff! A young piranha smells food from far away.

Piranhas have an amazing sense of smell. They can detect a single drop of blood in the water from far away. Their noses help them find food fast.

A special line runs along each side of a piranha's body. It is called a **lateral line**. This line feels tiny waves and vibrations in the water, even in total darkness.

With these skills, piranhas find meals in the murkiest rivers. They can also hear low sounds that travel through the water. Nothing escapes their notice.

STAY SAFE

Piranhas make a barking sound by grinding their teeth when they want to scare enemies away!

DID YOU KNOW?

Whoosh! A school of piranhas blend into the shadowy water on the river floor.

Piranhas have clever ways to stay safe. Their dark backs help them blend in with the river bottom. From above, predators cannot spot them easily.

Their bellies are lighter in color. This tricks animals looking up from below. The light belly blends in with the bright sky above the water.

Piranhas also have tough, bony scales. These scales act like tiny shields, protecting the fish from bites and scrapes. Their whole body is built for survival.

MORE THAN MEAT

Some piranhas eat so many seeds and fruits that they help spread new plants along the riverbanks!

Crunch! A wimple piranha nips a scale off another fish.

Piranhas eat much more than just meat. Many munch on fruits, seeds, and plants that fall into the water. They also gobble up bugs and small fish.

The wimple piranha has a very strange diet. It sneaks up on other fish and bites off their scales! The scales give it the protein it needs to survive.

Most piranhas are **omnivores**. That means they eat both plants and animals. They are not nearly as scary as movies make them seem.

FEEDING FRENZY

Thrash! The water boils as piranhas rush in for a meal.

Red-bellied piranhas are famous for feeding frenzies. When food runs low, many piranhas rush in to eat at once. The water shakes and splashes like a boiling pot!

Each fish darts in for a quick bite. Then it swims away. It circles back for more. This way, every fish gets a turn at the meal.

But feeding frenzies do not happen often. Most of the time, piranhas eat on their own. They are usually calm and quiet hunters.

BIG BULLIES

DID YOU KNOW?

Giant river otters hunt in family groups and can catch and eat several piranhas in a single day!

Gulp! A piranha spots a caiman lurking in the shallows.

Even tough piranhas have enemies. Caimans are big reptiles that love to eat them. These large hunters sit and wait in the water, still as logs.

River dolphins also catch piranhas. Herons and other big birds swoop down and grab them from above. Even larger fish will gulp a piranha whole.

Piranhas must always watch out. Danger can come from above, below, or the side. Life in the river is full of risk for these little fish.

QUICK ESCAPE

Piranhas are most scared of big shadows moving above the water—it usually means a hungry bird!

Zoom! A scared piranha zips behind a tangle of roots.

When danger is near, piranhas act fast. They dart into thick plants or hide behind rocks. Speed is their best escape plan.

A piranha can change direction in a flash. Its thin body slips between tight spaces with ease. Tangled roots and branches make the best hiding spots.

Piranhas are very hard to catch. Their quick moves and good hiding spots keep them safe. A smart piranha always stays close to cover.

SWIFT SWIMMERS

When scared, a piranha can swim up to 15 miles per hour—about as fast as a person can run!

Whizz! A piranha shoots through the current like a dart.

Piranhas are fast and powerful swimmers. They push through the water with their wide tail fin. Short bursts of speed help them catch food or escape danger.

A piranha uses all its fins to steer. Side fins help it turn and stop quickly. The tail fin gives it the power to zoom ahead in an instant.

Black piranhas are some of the fastest. They live in swift rivers with strong **currents**, so swimming fast helps them keep up with the flow.

DAY LIFE

DID YOU KNOW?
Piranhas keep their favorite spots in the river and will chase away any fish that swims too close!

Gurgle! A gold piranha wakes up and starts its busy day.

Piranhas are busiest in the early morning and late afternoon. They spend this time looking for food. When the sun is high and hot, they rest in the shade.

At dawn, piranhas patrol their part of the river. They check for food and watch for danger. Some nibble on plants along the way.

As the sun sets, they feed again. Then they settle into calm, shallow water for the night. Tomorrow, the routine starts all over.

SCHOOL SQUAD

FUN FACT!

Some piranha schools have more than 100 fish swimming side by side—imagine that traffic jam!

Swish! Dozens of piranhas glide through the water together.

Red-bellied piranhas live in groups called **schools**. A school often has 20 to 30 fish. There is safety in numbers!

Piranhas in a school swim together and watch for trouble. If a predator gets close, the group moves as one. Together, they can look like one big, scary fish.

Being in a school also helps with finding food. More eyes means more chances to spot a meal. The whole group benefits when one fish finds something tasty.

FINDING LOVE

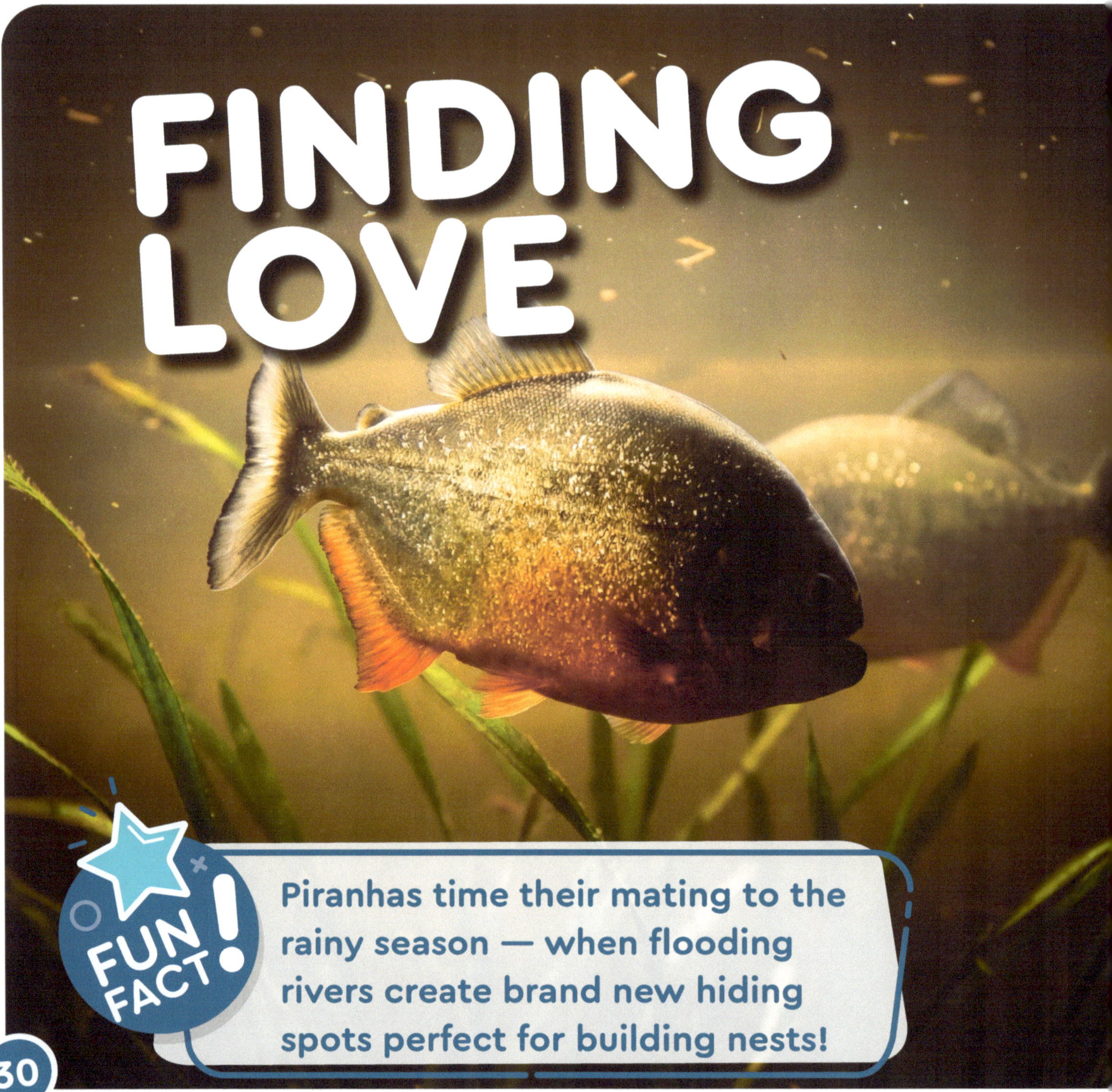

FUN FACT!

Piranhas time their mating to the rainy season — when flooding rivers create brand new hiding spots perfect for building nests!

Swirl! Two piranhas circle each other in a special water dance.

When it is time to mate, piranhas put on a show. Males turn a deeper, brighter color to catch a female's eye. The more vivid the color, the better the chance of finding a partner.

A pair of piranhas swims in wide circles together, chasing and nudging each other through the water. This courtship dance can go on for hours before a female makes her choice.

Once she is ready, the female finds a safe spot near plant roots or a sheltered bank to lay her eggs. The male stays close to guard them.

TINY FRY

DID YOU KNOW?
A piranha fry is about the size of a grain of rice when it hatches—tinier than your pinky nail!

Swish! A tiny piranha baby swims along the river floor.

Baby piranhas are called **fry**. They hatch from tiny, clear eggs. Each egg is smaller than a pea!

A mother piranha can lay up to 5,000 eggs at once. The eggs stick to plants and roots under water. In just two to three days, the fry start to hatch.

Baby fry are very small and almost see-through. They eat tiny bugs and bits of plants to grow strong. Within weeks, they start to look like their parents.

DAD DUTY

Piranha dads barely eat while guarding eggs—they refuse to leave the nest even for a quick snack!

34

Flap! A father piranha guards his nest from a passing fish.

Father piranhas are the main nest guards. The male watches over the eggs day and night. He chases away any fish that comes too close!

The father also fans the eggs with his fins. This keeps clean water flowing over them. Fresh water helps the eggs grow strong and healthy.

Once the babies hatch, the father stays near. He guards the fry until they can swim well on their own. Then they join the school and start their own adventures.

BUILT TOUGH

Piranhas can survive in water with very little oxygen—conditions that would kill most other fish!

Splish! A piranha swims through a shallow stream to find deeper water.

Piranhas are built to survive tough times. When rivers dry up, they move to deeper pools. They wait there until the rain returns.

Piranhas are also surprisingly tough on the inside. They heal quickly from wounds, even bites from other piranhas. Their bodies fight off infection fast.

Their strong jaws and sharp senses keep them alive in dangerous waters. That's why piranhas have lasted for such a long time. They are true survivors of the Amazon.

UP CLOSE!
FUN FACT!
People in South America have been fishing for piranhas for thousands of years—and some even keep them as pets!
38

Wow! A school of piranhas glides past the glass at an aquarium.

You do not need to travel to the Amazon to see a real piranha. Many zoos and aquariums keep them in large tanks. Press your face to the glass and watch them glide past — those teeth are the real deal!

Piranhas are actually calmer than most people expect. In a tank, they often swim slowly in a group, turning together like one smooth machine.

Next time you visit an aquarium, find the piranha tank. Watch them closely. You might just walk away with a whole new respect for these incredible fish!

GLOSSARY

fry
Baby fish that have just hatched from eggs.

school
A group of fish that swim together.

lateral line
A line on a fish's body that senses waves in water.

omnivore
An animal that eats both plants and animals.

current
The steady flow of water moving in one direction through a river or ocean